A MOTLEY TO THE VIEW

Allen Bell

Bayeux Arts

BAYEUX ARTS
119 Stratton Crescent S.W.
Calgary, Alberta, Canada T3H 1T7

CANADIAN CATALOGUING IN PUBLICATION DATA

Bell, Allen.
    A Motley To The View

    Poems.
    ISBN 1-896209-80-7

    I. Title
PS8553.E4555M67 2002   C811'.6   C2002-910523-4
PR9199.3.B37726M67 2002

The publisher gratefully acknowledges the generous support of
The Canada Council for the Arts, The Alberta Foundation for the
Arts and the Government of Canada through the Book Publishing
Industry Development Program.

Cover Photo: Lynda Gammon

Printed and bound in Canada

Also by Allen Bell

The Simon Poems

Thy Harry's Company

Puppet Poems

A Motley To The View [1981-1984]

Simon was watching television
And saw an American Presidential Candidate's
Advertisement
What does he mean
Well politicians like to talk about all the things they say will happen if they are elected
And this person is saying that if he gets the job
He won't hurt anybody
He won't make war
Oh good
Then I hope he gets it
Then there wouldn't be war with that man

LOVE

Sometimes I wish that I could fuck a fish
Or hump a whale
Or goose a moose
Or eat a cow
One could learn how

Love
Teaches us
To forego
Slaughter and experimentation
And read Peter Singer et al
And not do almost unto other species
That which we do unto our own

CRUISE SHIPS

Sometimes I travel
On freighters
And cruise ships
E.g., the Queen Elizabeth
And while still extant
The France
And the food
And the women
Make me hallucinate
And see a world
Of fantasy
And make-believe
It is all one can do to guard against herpes
But eventually the opulence would pall
One would get sick
And unable to cope
With crapulous days
And sex
The ship was a vomitorium
And brothel
And I would stay in my cabin
With the door locked
And lie in bed
And spit on the wall
Like Goncharov's Oblomov

THE LOVE SONG OF J. ALBERT PIERREPOINT

Sometimes I think about batch strangulation
And the white or black hood
To mask the agony
And facial contortions
And I think of our English method
Which I perfected
A Royal Commission queried me
Re same
The English method is foolproof
I said
And cannot be improved
I said
Provided an experienced man
Does the job
The knot, I pointed out, is the bottom line
And must be under the angle of the left jaw
Otherwise the knot finishes behind the neck
I.e., strangulation
Whereas the knot
On the left-hand side
Finishes in front
And throws the chin back
And breaks the spinal cord
I was asked about the drop
Where the person stands
If that is important
I don't think so
I said
The knot is the criterion
And must be on the left lower jaw
And if the knot is on that side
Then when the person falls

The knot will finish
Under the chin
And throw the chin back
But the knot
On the right-hand side
Would finish up
Behind one's neck
And throw the neck forward
And make a strangulation
Field Marshal Keitel
Is alleged
To have lived
Twenty-four minutes
On the rope
At Nuremberg
And Hermann Goering
Told his American Army chaplain
Mr. Gerecke
He was convinced
His hanging
Would last fifteen minutes
I have hanged several people myself
He said
And I know the procedure
The hangman will make the knot somewhat loose
And I shall be slowly strangled
And Mr. Gerecke said
That was why the Reichmarschall
Ingested poison

*

I linger
In the chambers
Of the mind
With myriad sea-girls
Moribund and blind
And hear their sundry voices
Scream and lie
And then I pull the lever
And we die

NORAH

Sometimes I think that the biological syndrome is misleading
That the source of intelligence is radioactive material
That the radioactivity
That nullifies us
May, in time, regenerate us
So because of a tenuous
And, perhaps, desperate
Hope
I view
With a modicum
Of equanimity
And a degree
Of resignation
What appears to be an irreversible process
But I am also appalled
By the potential manner
Of our respective deaths
And the deaths of our children
Though our intimacy per se
Has already died
In the hurly burly of your life
In the mute commands of your omnipotent husband
Your demented job
Your selfish guilt
And the feeling that once consumed us
Has become for you
A nuisance
An irritant
Something to suppress
A mutant
Warped, nasty, disfigured
And your conversation
Once so loving and looked forward to

A sub-text
But the truth is
I like it when you itemize my faults
And tell me what I know is wrong with me
And belabour the conduct you say you always secretly belittled
Your voice caresses me
Your remote body penetrates me
And as I watch
The process
By which you begin
To phase me
Out of your life
Sad eyes beseeching
I see again the blossoming woman
Who came to fruition
On my bed

PARIS

I went to Paris
And ingested
And imbibed
And sundry social activities
And sightseeing
Even the sewers (Les Egouts)
As well as the catacombs
I had a wonderful time
I went to Paris
In an effort
To put some distance
Between us
And I did
I put some distance
Between us
And now
I don't even think about you anymore
I don't even like you anymore
I eat
And sleep
And get on with my life
As if I were in Paris
Admittedly
When I'm in a restaurant
I notice
I'm looking
At someone
Other than you
And when I sleep
I can't control my dreams
But other than the aforementioned
Everything is fine
Almost Parisian

THE MUSTARD SEED SOCIETY

I went to the Mustard Seed Society
In Victoria, British Columbia, Canada
For a turkey dinner
Gratis
And four hundred indigent Victorians
Accompanied me
But before we received
Our free turkey dinner
We heard about Jesus
How he came to a world that rejected his message
How he suffered and was crucified
How we are celebrating his birth
How the dinner was being bestowed upon us
In his name
How those who believe in him
Are saved
But those who reject his message
Are doomed to eternal perdition
I thought of Torquemada
And the messages
Of other centuries
And I thought of the messages
Of this century
And the nuclear terminus
To all messages
In all centuries
A lot of perdition
And indubitably eternal
And while my mind was saturated with messages
Theocratic messages
Ideological messages
The guest opposite me
(five elongated tables stretching the length of the hall)

Said hey this is good stuff
And I noticed my dinner
And tasted same
And the good stuff appellation was apropos
Turkey and homemade stuffing
And carrots
Cooked in the juices of the turkey
And potatoes
Dampened in the turkey's gravy
And cranberry sauce
One's plate was replete
And the turkey per se
Was gargantuan
A substantial repast
And not the least bit bogus
This was not cafeteria food
One's most optimistic expectations
Had been transcended
The guest adjacent to me
An Indian
Ingested noisily
And with apparent zest and gusto
But he looked sad
And appeared to be knowledgeable
Re suffering
And crucifixion
One could see where the nails had gone in
So to speak
Certainly, facially, a godawful mess
Gloucester after III.vii
An eye
And, also, an ear
Were not especially aesthetic

A nose approximated crushed tomato
And, also, scars
One ugly streak
At time of infliction
Must have cut his throat
I alluded to same
And inquired half-jokingly
If he'd been tortured
He said he'd been in knife fights
With white guys
And a lot of other crap he said
But he was through with that shit
Jesus had saved him
But that was not why he'd accepted the Society's public invitation
He'd come because he was damn hungry
Our waiter
A jolly gentleman
Dressed in red
Said to a man who seemed to be in charge of the proceedings
From maitre d' to waiter
And the man looked up
And smiled
Our Lord wants us to talk to them
And suffer for them
Think of what the saints did
And the maitre d'/waiter said
I'm trying to keep that in mind
Dinner was receding
And the speaker again said
Ladies and gentlemen can I have your attention please
And he said something about the Mustard Seed Society having prepared a wonderful dess
Apple pie with real apples

But first . . .
But people were talking
And a few had decamped
(I heard one man say he wasn't that hungry
And saw him get up and leave
And a mother told her children
To hurry
And finish eating
So they could all go home)
And in the general mêlée
The speaker's words were indistinct
I'm a slow eater
And was in the process of putting more cranberry sauce
On the residue
Of my turkey
And as the speaker talked
And the room emptied
I regretted the paucity of condiments
That was my message
I wanted more condiments
A modicum
Of mustard
O reason not the need
I wanted some mustard
To season my turkey
And make that free meal
Almost edible

NIGEL

In the township of Dartford
In the county of Kent
A white horse
Stands on two legs
The horse is Invicta
The white horse of Kent
At Gravesend Grammar School
In the township of Dartford
In the county of Kent
They caned me
Every morning six of the best
I would bend over
And the Headmaster
His surname was Stevens
The boys called him Sir
Would slowly count each stroke
He opened his grandfather clock
Which was filled with canes
Choose a cane he said
And smiled
Six of the best
I bent over
My hands on his desk
And he caned me
I didn't do my homework
And each day he caned me
At night
I knew that when I awoke
I would be sent to the Headmaster
He would open his grandfather clock
Stevens his name was
I called him Sir
Once a history master

Who several years later became Gravesend's Headmaster
Caned me on my fingers
On nerve-endings
On scar tissue
Underneath a scab
And I bled
An older boy stood up
Don't do that Sir
And the teacher said sit down
Or you'll get the same
And they looked at each other
And the boy sat down
And I cried
Because I was grateful that someone had helped me
Because I was grateful that someone had stood up
Because of my gratitude
Stop it
I'm a little boy
Don't hurt me
And when they gradually saw he was funny
They expelled me
And my grandfather disowned me
And after multiple difficulties
I travelled to Canada
Where I live somewhat close to the knuckle
But I do my homework
And study
And they cane me
But I draw the human figure
I always draw the human figure
I'm learning to draw the human figure
Stop it
Stop it

Stop it
Stop it I cry
And I think of Invicta
In the township of Dartford
In the county of Kent
Where Gravesend . . .
There is a white horse
Standing on two legs
The horse is Invicta
The white horse of Kent
The statue at Dartford
I think of Invicta
The white horse
The white horse
Standing
On two legs

SABY

Cavorting on Moss Street
And Linden Avenue
Barking
Chasing birds
Running so fast
One could not even begin to keep up
But always -- always coming back
For Susan's requisite pat and 'good girl'
Susan's friend and companion
Lying under her bed at night
And by the desk in her office during the day
And waiting outsides stores when she was shopping
Always together
Car, ferry
And the countless walks
Saby spotting a bird
Careering out of sight
Believing one can embark on adventitious quests
With impunity
Because birds never fall
To the earth
Then suddenly reappearing
Tongue hanging out
Homing in on her Susan
Even in the dark days of Castlegar
The indefatigable Saby
Exuded life
As she ran around the circular mile track
In Kinnaird Park
And we ran with her
And when we were out of breath
And had to pause
And separate

And Susan went on ahead
Saby kept looking back
As if expecting me to catch up
And unable to comprehend
Why I was falling behind
Then on to Victoria
And protective of Simon
And jumped on me
And licked my face
And lay on her back
During the sporadic visitations
And Susan and Saby loved one another
And if Susan was sad or mad
Saby was more agitated
Than Inga and Terza
The cats who loved her
And of whom she was also fond
And who are now Susan's only animals
Because Saby was uncomfortable
Her body as strong as ever
But her nose bleeding
A tumor likely malignant
The blood would bother her sometimes
And the cortisone made her sleepy
And before cancer gutted her body
Susan put her to sleep
She lay on Susan's lap
And Susan talked to her
And she didn't even feel the final needle
Because her world had always revolved around Susan
And when Susan talked she was oblivious of distractions
The drug overpowered her
And Saby fluttered -- fluttered away

THE PLACE

The right place to be in the world
The archetypal dwelling
And thryes hadde she been at Jerusalem
She hadde passed many a straunge strem
At Rome she hadde been, and at Boloigne
In Galice at Seint Jame, and at Coloigne
She coude muche of wandring by the weye
But the ubiquitous self prevails
And one studies geology
Rocks and fossils
Emotionless
Petrified and extant
One needn't cope with feelings
Whereas pre-nuclear people
Are redolent of emotion
And they make demands
And life per se makes demands
I thought I would find the place where I'd enjoy living
Where I would be happy so to speak
But the world is an island
And global parameters keep one enthralled
And even if one found another planet
And had the technological wherewithal to become domiciled therein
The self, of course, is not a Siamese twin
Cut and jettisoned
A locale palls
A geographical cure is not tenable
And one remains on one's island
And studies . . . geology
And learns the appropriate . . . terminology

SOMETIMES/MY NAMESAKE*

Sometimes I think of my namesake
The painter
His 'success' did not preempt
Self-slaughter
And I think of Chief Joseph
Of the Nez Perce
He said I will fight no more forever
And I think of other Indians
Spoiled lives
Squandered generations
And I think of myself
And sometimes I look in a mirror
And I see the stereotyped image
The drunk Indian
The dumb Indian
The misfit
The interloper
The deadbeat
The loser
The transplanted Thersites
The forgotten Hector
And I say to myself what has this to do with me
But it is this image I sometimes . . . perceive
And sometimes -- sometimes . . . believe

*I entered a 'literary contest' under the pseudonym Benjamin Joseph.
The reference is to Benjamin Chee Chee.

STOCKS

Sometimes I think about stocks
Whether to buy long
Or sell short
A gargantuan roulette wheel
And one must choose numbers
And make money
And many people lose money
(And I have lost money)
And some go the route
Of Dostoevsky's compulsive protagonist
But profit or loss notwithstanding
A perception of bondage
Keeps one enthralled
I look at presidents
And other politicians
And read the business section
Of the Globe and Mail
And watch news
On television
And listen to commentaries
And sometimes I watch the proceedings
From my stall in Grub Street
And on Sunday
I stare at a football game
And the owners of America
Chortle

SOPHIA

But shall I live in hope?
All men, I hope, live so.
(Shakespeare)

Jews
And then to an even greater extent
Christians
Split the world
And the passion
For power
And dominion
Predominates
And now we are up to our armpits in gasoline
And the elite play with matches
But I will still fantasize
And embrace Sophia
And she takes me to her room
And I lie in the center of her bed
And she embraces me
And the whole Judeo-Christian catastrophe fucks off
And the impending apocalypse gradually recedes
And we embrace her
And impregnate her
And she renews
And anima calms the world
And there is light

THAT CIGAR

My first job was the University of Saskatchewan
Saskatoon campus
And I wrote a paper entitled
The American Invasion of South Vietnam
Which I sent to faculty staff students
And a week later
I received a phone call
From the secretary
Of the chairman
Of my department
And was summoned
And faculty had phoned him
And Political Science was up in arms
And complaints
From students
And parents
And a few hours later
I received a long distance phone call
And was advised
To cool it
This was my career
And a few days later
I was playing chess
In the faculty lounge
And an American academic
Approached me
And pounded the chessboard
And scattered the pieces
And told me what he thought of me
And what he would do to me if I sent him anything else
And insofar as I could understand him
I had transgressed the parameters

Of discussion
And was so far out of the margins I didn't exist
And after that incident
I was shunned
But then the complaints stopped
Though there were other papers
And they were distributed
And that was my last year
And years later
I left academe
Tired and jaundiced
And somewhat reclusive
And several months later approached me
And was sitting on a sofa
At the faculty club
And sat beside me
And sipped scotch
And smoked a huge cigar
And after several minutes
Of thought and reflection
You know
You're crazy
But everything you write is publishable

OBITER DICTUM

When I was in Amnesty
I wrote a lot of letters
But epistolary appearances notwithstanding
I pissed against the wind
Shakespeare: O Goneril
You are not worth the dust
Which the rude wind
Blows in your face
And when our Group-in-Formation
Disbanded
And I lost my motley of misfits
Simon: Why are you a weirdo Daddy
I decided to throw in the towel
But while I was in Amnesty
My job was Latin America
Arguably the world's worst torture chamber
So my focal point was torture
And what with epistolic endeavours and so forth
I suppose I was somewhat knowledgeable
And even by America's Latin American standards
Somoza's National Guard
Was noteworthy
And I was nonplussed when the propaganda system talked about freedom fighters
And revolutionaries
Just because the NG was being rearmed under American auspices
And given carte blanche to wreak havoc
(Which as of the date of this poem they are certainly doing)
And I recall an interview
That I transcribed for Amnesty
To which I listened in awe
Because the interviewee talked about what he was doing
And resembled a pilot who said he didn't like dropping napalm
on Vietnamese women and children
Because of what it did to them he said

And he seemed exasperated
As if what he was doing was so obvious that even a dumb journalist could conceptua
Do you think this is a game he said
Go to Honduras
See the refugees
Talk to them
Maybe you'll learn something
This is not a game
This is war
You'll see some of the things we do
I don't like doing them
Especially women
Some of the guys do but I don't
We have to
Because we need information
And if a guy's mind doesn't go
We get it
We use electricity of course
Testicles nipples you know
And blowtorches under their armpits
And nails
And toe nails
But some of those guys are really tough
So we pop out their eyes with spoons
When we do women
I listened to this recounting
Of his sponsored activities
But the words ceased to be audible
Though I heard the sound
And I was transported
But I heard the sound
And I was naked

In a shower
Without water

SYNAGOGUE

When one is young
One goes with one's parents
And I often went to the synagogue
And on one occasion
Money was being pledged to Israel
And there were several speakers
And one speaker said he had lived in Germany
And had been sent to the Buchenwald concentration camp
And had survived
And his wife and all his children had not survived
And he had moved to Israel
And had made a success
And remarried
And he was now visiting his grandchildren in Canada
And he said he could never have imagined in Buchenwald
That one day he would live in a Jewish country
This was beyond his dreams
And he said in Israel
He had found a home
He had found freedom and dignity
And not contempt
And death
In Buchenwald he said
He was concerned with survival
But afterwards
He discovered
That when he left Buchenwald
He was still trying to survive
And was suffering
And ate so much he almost killed himself
And he said Israel had assuaged his suffering
And enabled him to survive

And he thanked God
That unlike so many Jewish people
He survived the holocaust
And experienced Israel
And he said Israel's survival depends on you
And the congregation looked at him as if with one face
And as he was leaving the pulpit
An old man passed him
And took his place
And he was not a scheduled speaker
And he said he had worked hard
But was not successful
And as the English writer William Shakespeare said in his play for the theatre
King Lear
He did not have bags of money
For his children
And they did not respect him
And sometimes abused him
And were making him unhappy
But he didn't care
Because for many years he had worshipped in God's synagogue
And was rich beyond all measure
And I heard the word mishooga
And there were murmurings
Because the subject was Israel
And people had come to hear
And to talk about
And no one wanted to listen to
The synagogue's eccentric
And he said a synagogue is inviolate
And can be defaced
And spat upon

And burned to the ground
But cannot be desecrated
And he said during the pogroms
And deprivation
And slaughter
The churches said nothing
That religion said nothing
And we raise money for Israel in a synagogue
And say nothing
Palestinians he said
And he repeated
Palestinians
Who are people
Who have children
Who should not be dispossessed
And demeaned
And made scapegoats
They are the Jews
And we are the Germans
And Christians
And suddenly he pointed to the man who had lived in Germany
You, especially, he said
You you you
You cannot only love Nazis
And the rabbi got up
And there were shouts
And then
In a feeble but strangely audible voice
That was heard throughout the synagogue
Go back to Israel
Marshal the survivors of the holocaust
Establish a moral force

That the military juggernaut
Cannot trample
And he said Israel is an obscenity
And will move from horror to horror
And walked down from the pulpit
And into the congregation
And stopped in front of the preceding speaker
And the man from Buchenwald stood up
And the two survivors
Embraced
And I was close by
And saw tears

*Issam Sartawi was shot by an unknown assailant (April 10, 1983) while attending a conference in Albufeira, Portugal. There is no evidence whats that this scenario was orchestrated by the Mossad.

WHEN THE MOSSAD MURDERED SARTAWI*

Countries opt for what they conceive to be strength
And their secret police
Receive assignments
And also work elsewhere
And one becomes inured
To a modus operandi
One sometimes hears about
After facts are rearranged
And distorted
But when the Mossad murdered Sartawi
I was surprised
Because their prime minister said they don't pose a military threat
In fact he said militarily they're negligible
But he said they pose a very serious political threat
And Sartawi embodied
That threat
Because he endeavoured to persuade
And could not be characterized
And was moderate
And talked about compromise
And peace
And, in a larger sense,
Symbolized sanity
And I was surprised
Because his sense of humour
Was Swiftian
And he said countries have a penchant
For territory
And although Lilliputian

Are imperial
And he said morality
In politics
Is a misnomer
And moral degeneracy is a drop in the bucket
And he said the direction . . .
And this country is symptomatic
And he was civilized
And a humanist
And eschewed war
And talked about peace
And endeavoured to persuade
And was too disconcerting
So someone stood behind him
And fired point blank
And I was surprised
And the bullet
That smashed his head
And shattered his brain
And stilled his voice
Murdered centuries

SI VIS PACEM,

The state religion is sacrosanct
But totalitarian countries bludgeon
Whereas western democracies lobotomize

MONKEY

When I was a teenager
I often went to the movies
And still do to some extent
And saw a film called Primate
Directed by Frederick Wiseman
And this director was a beautiful stylist
Spare and elegant
And very rigorous
And there was a musical quality
And there was a crystallizing simplicity
And I would have liked to have seen his other films
But was never able to do so
And had to be content, for the most part, with Hollywood gibberish
But I was somewhat shocked by his weltanschauung
Because he seemed to believe
We had created concentration camps
And that animals pay an incredibly exorbitant price
For our experiments
And our subsequent
Technology
And I especially disliked
The startling juxtaposition
Of monkey and rocket
Because he seemed to believe
That the price
That our own species
Was paying
Was not retractable

Simon was watching television
And saw an American Presidential Candidate's
Advertisement
What does he mean
Well politicians like to talk about all the things they say will happen if they are ele
And this person is saying that if he gets the job
He won't hurt anybody
He won't make war
Oh good
Then I hope he gets it
Then there wouldn't be war with that man